# Inner Wisdom

## Meditations for the Heart and Soul

### Louise L. Hay

Hay House, Inc.
Carlsbad, California • Sydney, Australia

*Published and distributed in the United States by:*
Hay House, Inc., P.O. Box 5100, Carlsbad, CA 92018-5100
(800) 654-5126 • (800) 650-5115 (fax)

*Editorial:* Jill Kramer • *Cover and interior design:* Christy Salinas
*Illustrations:* Eris Klein

### Library of Congress Cataloging-in-Publication Data

Hay, Louise L.
    Inner wisdom / Louise L. Hay.
      p. cm.
    ISBN 1-56170-729-5
      1. Meditations. 2. Affirmations. I. Title.

BL624.2.H377 2000
291.4'32—dc21

                                      99-059129

Some of the material in this book was originally published in
*Heart Thoughts* © 1990 by Louise L. Hay.

ISBN 1-56170-729-5

03 02 01 00     4 3 2 1
1st printing, August 2000

Printed in China through Palace Press International

# Introduction

by Louise L. Hay

Within each of us is a center of wisdom far deeper and greater than we are aware of. The meditations in this book are designed to help us connect with that center and magnify our understanding of life. When we are willing to open our consciousness to new ideas and new ways of thinking about issues, then our lives change for the better. The only goal I really have is to continually grow in understanding—to understand more about life and how it works. What do I need to know, believe, say, and do to make my life flow as smoothly as possible?

Within each of us is the capability to connect with our source, and there lies the peace we are all seeking—the inner knowledge that gives us strength in the so-called dark times. When we can see the larger picture of life, we also see how insignificant many of the smaller issues we have are. We truly understand the saying; "Don't sweat the small stuff; it is *all* small stuff."

Every time we say "I don't know," we are shutting down the doors to our own infinite source of wisdom. Within us are all the answers to all the questions we shall ever ask. We do know past, present, and future. Among us are gifted psychics, and if one person can do something, we can all do it. We all have the potential to know more, to see more, to understand more, and to see the greater picture of life.

The way we begin our day sets the tone for the experiences that will follow and how we will react to them. A good way to use this book is to open it at random first thing in the morning. Know that the meditation you choose is the perfect message for that day. I also like to close my day with uplifting thoughts. It is a good way to have pleasant dreams and to awaken clearheaded in the morning.

Remember, in the vast infinity of life, all is perfect, whole, and complete . . . and so are you.

— *Louise L. Hay*

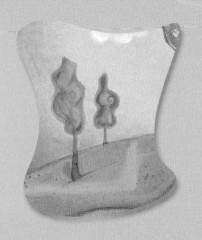

I am
a Yes
person

I know I am one with all of life. I am surrounded and filled with infinite wisdom. Therefore, I rely totally on the Universe to support me in every positive way. I was created by life and was given this planet to fulfill all my needs. Everything I could possibly need is already here waiting for me. No matter what I choose to believe or think or say, the Universe always says yes to me. I do not waste my time on negative thinking or negative subjects. I choose to see myself and life in the most positive ways. Therefore, I say yes to opportunity and prosperity. I say yes to all good. I am a yes person living in a yes world, being responded to by a yes Universe, and I rejoice that this is so.

# I am centered in truth and peace

No matter where I am, there is only Spirit, God, infinite good, infinite wisdom, infinite harmony, and love. It cannot be otherwise. There is no duality. There are no problems that do not have a solution. There are no questions without answers. I now choose to go beyond the problem to seek the Divine right-action solution to any discord that may seem to appear in the true harmonious atmosphere of my world. I am willing to learn and grow from this seeming discord and confusion. I release all blame, and turn within to seek the truth. I declare for myself and for each and every person in my life: peace, security, harmony, a deep sense of love for the self, and the willingness to love others. I am centered in truth, and I live in joy.

# I heal myself on all levels

This is a time of compassion and a time of healing. I go within and connect with that part of myself that knows how to heal. It is possible. I know that I am in the process of healing. During this time, I discover my healing abilities—abilities that are strong and powerful. I am incredibly capable. I am willing to go to a new level to truly heal myself on all possible levels. I am spirit, and being spirit, I am free to help myself—and the world.

# I accept all the parts of myself

The biggest part of healing and making myself whole is to accept all of the many parts of myself. I accept the times when I did well, and the times when I didn't do so well; the times when I was terrified, and the times when I was loving; the times when I was very foolish and silly, and the times when I was very bright and clever; the times when I had egg on my face, and the times when I was a winner. All of these are parts of myself. Most of my problems come from rejecting parts of myself—not loving myself totally and unconditionally. I do not look back on my life with shame. I look at the past as part of the richness and fullness of life. Without this richness and fullness, I would not be here today. When I accept all of myself, I become whole and healed.

# I let my whole being vibrate with light

I look deep within the center of my heart and find that tiny pinpoint of brilliantly colored light. It is such a beautiful color. It is the very center of my love and healing energy. I watch as my pinpoint of light begins to pulsate and grow until it fills my heart. I let it move through my body from the top of my head to the tips of my toes and through the tips of my fingers. I am absolutely glowing with this beautiful colored light, which is my love and healing energy. I say to myself: *With every breath I take, I'm getting healthier and healthier*. I feel the light cleansing my body of dis-ease. I let the light radiate from me into my special place in the world.

# Every hand that touches me is a healing hand

I am a precious being and loved by the Universe. As I increase the love I have for myself, so too does the Universe mirror this, increasing love ever more abundantly. I know that the Universal Power is everywhere—in every person, place, and thing. This loving, healing power flows through the medical profession and is in every hand that touches my body. I attract only highly evolved individuals on my healing pathway. My presence helps to bring out the spiritual, healing qualities in each practitioner. Doctors and nurses are amazed at their abilities to work as a healing team with me.

I am taking the next step for my healing

When I make an affirmation such as this one, I know that it is a beginning point. It opens the way. I am saying to my subconscious mind: *I am taking responsibility. I am aware there is something I can do to change.* If I continue to say the affirmation, I will either be ready to let whatever it is go, and the affirmation will become true; or it will open a new avenue to me. I may get a brilliant brainstorm, or a friend my call me and say, *Have you ever tried this?* I will be led to the next step that will help me with my healing.

# My home is a peaceful haven

My home is a reflection of me, so I now decide to "clean house." I clean my closets and refrigerator. I take all the clothes that I haven't worn in a period of time and sell them, give them away, or burn them. I get rid of the old so that I can make room for the new. As I let it go, I say: *I'm cleaning the closets of my mind.* I do the same with my refrigerator. I clean out all the foods and scraps that have been there for a while. I know that people who have very cluttered closets and cluttered refrigerators have cluttered minds. So, I make my home a wonderful place to live in.

# My income
## is constantly
# increasing

I know that the quickest way to increase my income is to do the mental work first. In order to help myself be more prosperous, I can either choose to attract or repel money and other forms of prosperity. Complaining never works. I have a cosmic mental bank account, and I can deposit positive affirmations and believe I deserve, or believe that I do not. I affirm: *My income is constantly increasing. I have abundance in all areas of my life.* I find that I attract prosperity with ease.

I am
always
perfectly
protected

Sometimes when my life is going magnificently well, I get anxious, wondering if something bad is going to happen to take it all away. I know that anxiety is fear and not trusting myself, so I just recognize it as the part that is used to my being upset about something, thank it for sharing, and let it go. When I become frightened, my adrenalin pumps up to protect me from danger. I say to the fear: *I appreciate that you want to help me.* Then I do an affirmation about that particular fear. I acknowledge and thank the fear, but I don't give it importance.

# I have unlimited potential

In the infinity of Life where I am, I rejoice in knowing that I am one with the Power that created me. This Power loves all Its creations, including me. I am a beloved child of the Universe and have been given everything. I am the highest form of life on this planet and have been equipped with all that I need for every experience I shall have. My mind is always connected to the One Infinite Mind; therefore, all knowledge and wisdom are available to me. I rejoice in my unlimitedness and know that before me lies the totality of possibilities in every area. I trust totally in the One Power, and I know that all is well in my world.

# I love myself
## totally in
### the now

Love is the biggest eraser there is. Love erases even the deepest imprinting because love goes deeper than anything. If my childhood imprinting was very strong and I keep saying: *It's all their fault,* then I can't change. I stay stuck. So, I do a lot of mirror work. I look at my reflection in the mirror and tell every part of my body and soul that I love it. I do this every morning when I wake up and every evening before I go to sleep. I love everything about this wonderful soul that is me.

I am
perfect
exactly
as I am

I am neither too much nor too little. I do not have to prove to anyone or anything who I am. I have been many identities, each one a perfect expression for that particular lifetime. I am content to be who and what I am this time. I do not yearn to be like someone else, for that is not the expression I chose this time. Next time I will be different. I am perfect as I am, right now. I am sufficient. I am one with all of life. There is no need to struggle to be better. All I need to do is love myself more today than yesterday, and to treat myself as someone who is deeply loved. With joy, I recognize my perfection and the perfection of life.

# I am willing to learn something new every day

When I recall my school days, I think, *Wouldn't it have been wonderful if, instead of having to memorize all those battle dates, my friends and I could have been taught how to think, how to love ourselves, how to have good relationships, how to be wise parents, how to handle money, and how to be healthy?* I can't change the past, but I can choose to learn all these things and more . . . today. I enrich my life by learning something new every day—and then teaching others what I know.

# I let go of the need for this condition in my life

I create habits and patterns because they serve me in some way. Sometimes I am punishing someone or loving someone. For example, it is amazing how many illnesses I've created because I wanted to punish a parent or love a parent. *I'm going to have diabetes just like my daddy, because I love my daddy.* It may not always be on a conscious level, but when I start looking within, I find the pattern. I often create negativity because I do not know how to handle some area of my life. I need to ask myself: *What am I feeling sorry about? Who am I angry at? What am I trying to avoid? How will this save me?* If I am not ready to let something go, it doesn't matter what I do; it just won't work. But when I *am* ready to let it go, it is amazing how the smallest thing can help me release it.

I create
wonderful
new
beliefs
for myself

These are some of the beliefs that I have created for myself over a period of time that really work for me:

I am always safe.

Everything I need to know is revealed to me.

Everything I need comes to me in the perfect time-space sequence.

Life is a joy and is filled with love.

I am always healthy and whole.

I prosper wherever I turn.

I am willing to change and grow.

All is well in my world.

# I am good enough

If there is any belief within me that says: *I can't have,* or *I'm not good enough,* I think to myself: *I am willing to let that belief go. I do not have to believe that anymore.* I don't have to struggle. It is not hard work. I am just changing a thought. I was born to enjoy life. I affirm that I am now willing to open to the abundance and prosperity that is available everywhere. I now claim this mentally for myself right here and right now: *I deserve to be prosperous. I deserve my good.* That which I have declared is already accomplished in consciousness and now becomes manifest in my experience. And so it is.

# My love is limitless

There is so much love in this world, and there is so much love in my heart, but sometimes I forget. Sometimes I think there isn't enough, or that there's just a small amount, so I hoard what I have or I am afraid to let it go. I am afraid to let it out. But then I realize that the more love I allow to flow out from me, the more there is within me and the more I receive. It is endless and timeless. Love is really the most powerful healing force that there is. Without love, I could not survive at all. Love heals, so I give it and accept it without limitation.

# My
## business
### is prosperous

I am Divinely guided, so my business prospers, expands, and grows. I now choose to release any negative thoughts about cash-flow limitations. I open my consciousness to a quantum leap of prosperity by thinking and accepting that large amounts of money flood to my bank account. I have plenty to use, to spare, and to share. The law of prosperity keeps the flow of cash moving in abundant amounts. It pays my bills and brings me everything I need and more. I now choose to be a living example of prosperity consciousness. I live and work in comfort and ease and beauty. I have inner peace and security. I watch with joy and gratitude as this business continually grows and prospers far beyond my expectations. I bless this business with love.

# I help create
# a world where
# it is safe for all
# of us to love
# each other

It is a dream of mine to help create a world where it is safe for all of us to love each other— where I can be loved and accepted exactly as I am. I realize that when I love myself, I don't hurt myself and I don't hurt other people. I let go of all prejudices and beliefs about one group or another not being good enough. When I realize how incredibly beautiful we all are, I have the answer to world peace—a world where it is safe for us to love each other. I help create this type of world with all the good I do every day.

# I rise above all limitations

Each experience is a stepping-stone in life, including any so-called mistakes. I love myself for all my mistakes and missteps. They have been very valuable to me. They have taught me many things. It is the way I learn. I am willing to stop punishing myself for my mistakes. Instead, I love myself for my willingness to learn and grow.

All of my changes are easy to make

When I begin to work on myself, sometimes things get worse before they get better. It is okay if that happens, because I know that it's the beginning of the process. It's untangling old threads. I just flow with it. It takes time and effort to learn what I need to learn. I don't demand instant change. Impatience is only resistance to learning. I let myself do it step by step. It will get easier as I go along.

# I am willing to see my magnificence

I now choose to eliminate from my mind and life every negative and destructive fearful idea and thought. I no longer listen to or become part of detrimental thoughts or conversations. Today, no one can harm me because I refuse to believe in being hurt. No matter how justified it may seem to be, I refuse to indulge in damaging emotions. I rise above anything that attempts to make me angry or afraid. Destructive thoughts have no power over me. I am more than adequate for all I need to do. I see only the magnificence that is me.

# This year I do the mental work for positive change

I know that until I make inner changes and am willing to do some mental work, nothing "out there" is going to change. The only thing I need to change is a thought—just a thought. So, this year, I think of all the positive things I can do for myself. I think only positive thoughts. I affirm what I want each day as soon as I wake up. I say, "Out" to any unwanted, negative thinking. I am grateful for all the good in my life. In this way, I do mental work that effects positive change.

# It's only
## a thought,
### and a thought
#### can be changed

How many times have I refused to think a positive thought about someone else? Well, I can refuse to think negative thoughts about myself, too. People say: *I can't stop thinking a thought.* Well, yes, I can. I have to make up my mind that that's what I'm going to do. I don't have to fight my thoughts when I want to change things. When that negative voice comes up, I can say: *Thank you for sharing.* I am not giving power over to the negative thought, and yet I am not denying that it is there. I am saying: *Okay, it's there, thank you for sharing, and I'm choosing to do something else. I don't want to buy into that anymore. I want to create another way of thinking.* I don't fight my thoughts. I acknowledge them and go beyond them.

# I am connected to all of life

I am spirit, light, energy, vibration, color, and love. I am so much more than I give myself credit for. I am connected with every person on the planet and with all of life. I see myself healthy, whole, and living in a society where it is safe for me to be who I am and to love others. I hold this vision for myself and for all of us, for this is a time of healing and making whole. I am part of that whole. I am one with all of life.

# I listen to my body's messages

In this world of change, I choose to be flexible in all areas. I am willing to change myself and my beliefs to improve the quality of my life and my world. My body loves me in spite of how I may treat it. My body communicates with me, and I now listen to its messages. I am willing to *get* the message. I pay attention and make the necessary adjustments. I give my body what it needs on every level to bring it back to optimum health. I call upon an inner strength that is mine whenever I need it.

I create
my future
now

No matter what my early childhood was like, the best or the worst, I am totally in charge of my life now. I can spend my time blaming my parents or my early environment, but all that accomplishes is keeping me stuck in victim patterns. It never gets me the good I say I want. My current thinking shapes my future. It can create a life of negativity and pain, or it can create a life of unlimited joy. I choose a bright future now.

# I open new doors to life

Ahead of me is a continuous corridor of doors—each one opening to a new experience. As I move forward, I see myself opening various doors on wonderful experiences that I would like to have. I trust that my inner guide is leading me and guiding me in ways that are best for me, and that my spiritual growth is continuously expanding. No matter which door opens or which door closes, I am always safe. I am eternal. I will go on forever from experience to experience. I see myself opening doors to joy, peace, healing, prosperity, love, understanding, compassion, forgiveness, freedom, self-worth, and self-esteem. It is all here before me.

# I allow others to be themselves

I cannot force others to change. I can offer them a positive mental atmosphere where they have the possibility to change if they wish, but I cannot do it *for* or *to* other people. Each person is here to work out his or her own lessons, and if I fix it for them, then they will just go and do it again, because they have not worked out what they needed to do for themselves. All I can do is love them, allow them to be who they are, and know that the truth is always within them and that they can change at any moment they want.

I communicate
openly with
my children

I keep the lines of communication open with my children, especially when they're in their teen years. I know that what often happens when children start to talk about things is that they are told over and over again: *Don't say this. Don't do that. Don't feel that. Don't be that way. Don't express that. Don't, don't, don't!* As a result, children stop communicating. I avoid these problems by listening, being open to my children's thoughts and ideas, and using compromise to handle challenging situations. My children and I forge a wonderful relationship.

# I am safe and secure in my world

When I feel insecure or frightened, I tend to pad my body with weight as a form of protection. I acknowledge that at these times, there is something going on in my life that is making me feel insecure. I can fight fat for 20 years and still be fat because I have not dealt with the underlying cause. If I am overweight, I put the weight issue aside and work on the other issue first—the pattern that says: *I need protection. I'm insecure.* However, I know not to get angry when the weight goes on, because my cells respond to my mental patterns. When the need for the protection is gone, or when I start feeling secure, the fat will melt off by itself. What I choose to think today will start creating my new figure tomorrow.

# I am
# worth loving

I don't have to earn love any more than I have to earn the right to breathe. I have a right to breathe because I exist. I have a right to be loved because I exist. I am worthy of my own love. I don't allow my parents' or society's negative opinions or popular prejudices to make me think that I am not good enough. The reality of my being is that I am lovable. I accept this and know this. I find that people now treat me as a lovable person.

I release
all feelings
of guilt

In the past, I lived under a heavy cloud of guilt. I always felt wrong. I wasn't doing it right. I was apologizing all the time. I wouldn't forgive myself for things I did in the past. I manipulated others as I once was manipulated. But now I know that guilt does not solve anything. If I did something in the past that I am sorry about, I stop doing it! If I can, I make amends to the other party. If I can't, I simply don't repeat the behavior. I'm aware that guilt looks for punishment, and punishment creates pain. So, I forgive myself, and I forgive others. I step out of my self-imposed prison.

# I keep my inner world peaceful

Because I keep myself centered in inner peace, I have peace in my outer world. Although others may have discord and chaos, it does not touch me, for I declare peace for myself. The Universe is one of great order and peacefulness, and I reflect this in every moment of my life. The stars and the planets do not need to be worried or fearful in order to maintain their heavenly orbits, nor does chaotic thinking contribute to my peaceful existence in life. I choose to express peacefulness, for I am peace.

# I speak and think positively

If I could understand the power of my words, I would be careful about what I say. I would talk constantly in positive affirmations. The Universe always says yes to whatever I say, no matter what I choose to believe. If I choose to believe that I am not very much, that life will never be any good, and that I will never get anything that I want, the Universe will respond, and that is exactly what I will have. The moment I start to change, the moment I am willing to bring good into my life, the Universe will respond in kind.

I look within my centered space and see the part of me that is pure spirit, pure light, and pure energy. I visualize all my limitations falling away one by one, until I am safe, healed, and whole. I know that no matter what is going on in my life, no matter how difficult things may be, at the very center of my being, I am safe and I am whole. I always will be. Lifetime after lifetime, I am a shining spirit—a beautiful light. Sometimes I come to this planet and cover my light and hide it, but the light is always there. As I let go of limitations, and as I recognize the true beauty of my being, I shine brilliantly. I am energy. I am the spirit of love shining brightly. I let my light shine.

# I am totally adequate at all times

I praise myself and tell myself how absolutely wonderful I am. I don't make myself wrong. When I do something new, I don't beat myself up just because I'm not a pro at it the first time. I practice; thereby learning what *does* work and what *doesn't* work. Next time I do something new or different, something I am just learning, I will be there for myself. I don't tell myself what was wrong with it; I tell myself what was right. I praise myself and build myself up so that the next time I do it, I really feel good about it. Each time I will be better and better and better. Soon I will have a new skill of some sort.

# I constantly receive incredible gifts

I learn to accept prosperity instead of exchanging it. If a friend gives me a gift or takes me to lunch, I don't have to immediately reciprocate. I allow the person to give me the gift. I accept it with joy and pleasure. I may never reciprocate to that person. I may give to someone else. If someone gives me a gift that I can't use or don't want, I say: *I accept this gift with joy and pleasure and gratitude,* and then I pass it on to someone else.

I love
being me

When I imagine how enjoyable it would be if I could live my life without ever being criticized by anyone, I think how totally at ease and comfortable I would feel. I would get up in the morning and know I was going to have a wonderful day, because everybody would love me, and nobody would judge me or put me down. I would just feel great. Well, I now realize that I can give this gift to myself. I can make the experience of living with myself the most fabulous experience imaginable. I can wake up in the morning loving myself, praising myself, and telling myself, "I love being me!"

# All of my relationships are enveloped in a circle of love

I envelop my fellow human beings in a circle of love, whether they are living or not. I include my friends, my family, my loved ones, my spouse, everyone from my work and my past, and all the people I would like to forgive and don't know how. I affirm that I have wonderful, harmonious relationships with everyone, where there is mutual respect and caring on both sides. I know that I can live with dignity and peace and joy. I let this circle of love envelop the entire planet, and I let my heart open so I can have a space within me filled with unconditional love. I am worth loving. I am beautiful. I am powerful. I open myself to all good.

# I am free and at peace

Today I am a new person. I relax and free my thoughts of every sense of pressure. No person, place, or thing can irritate or annoy me. I am at peace. I am a free person living in a world that is a reflection of my own love and understanding. I am not against anything. Rather, I am *for* everything that will improve the quality of my life. I use my words and my thoughts as tools to shape my future. I express gratitude and thanksgiving often, and I look for things to be thankful for. I am relaxed. I live a peaceful life.

I breathe in love, and I flow with life

Am I expanding or contracting? When I expand my thinking, my beliefs, and everything about me, the love flows freely. When I contract, I put up walls and shut myself off. If I am frightened or threatened or feel that something is just not right, I begin to breathe. Breathing opens me up. It straightens my spine. It opens my chest. It gives my heart room to expand. By practicing breathing, I drop the barriers and begin to open up. It is a beginning point. Instead of going into total panic, I take a few breaths and ask myself: *Do I want to contract, or do I want to expand?*

# I release all negative energy

No matter how long my negative beliefs have been in my subconscious, I affirm now that I am free of them. I affirm that I am willing to release the causes and patterns in my consciousness that are creating any negative conditions in my life. I affirm that I am now willing to release the need for any negative situations and conditions. I know that they disappear, fade away, and dissolve back into the nothingness from whence they came. The old garbage no longer has a hold on me. I am free!

# I let go of the past with ease, and I trust the process of life

I close the door on old, painful memories. I close the door on old hurts and old self-righteous unforgiveness. I might take an incident in the past where there was pain and hurt—something that is hard for me to forgive or look at. I ask myself: *How long do I want to hold on to this? How long do I want to suffer because of something that happened in the past*? Now I see a stream in front of me and take this old experience, this pain, this hurt, this unforgiveness, and put the whole incident in the stream and see it begin to dissolve and drift downstream until it totally dissipates and disappears. I *do* have the ability to let go.

# I
## deserve
# joy

I deserve to live in an atmosphere of joy and acceptance. I do daily affirmations in which I tell myself that I really deserve good and am willing to go beyond my parents' and my early childhood limitations. I look in the mirror and say to myself: *I deserve all good. I deserve to be prosperous. I deserve joy. I deserve love.* I open my arms wide and say: *I am open and receptive. I am wonderful. I accept.*

# I program my mind with positive thoughts

Reprogramming my negative beliefs is very powerful. A good way to do so is by making a tape with my own voice on it. My own voice means a lot to me. I make a tape of my affirmations and play it. It will have a great deal of value for me. If I want a tape that is even more powerful, I have my mother make a tape for me. I imagine going to sleep with my mother's voice telling me how wonderful I am, how much she loves me, how proud she is of me, and how she knows I can be *anything* in this world.

# I am motivated by love

I release from within me all bitterness and resentment. I affirm that I am totally willing to freely forgive everyone. If I think of anyone who may have harmed me in any way at any point in my life, I now bless that person with love and release him or her. I know that nobody can take anything from me that is rightfully mine. That which belongs to me will always return to me in Divine right order. If something does not come back to me, then it isn't meant to. I accept this idea with peace. Dissolving resentment is highly important. I trust myself. I am safe. I am motivated by love.

Everything I need comes to me in the perfect time-space sequence. Just as all the stars and planets are in their perfect orbit and in Divine right order, so am I. I may not understand everything that is going on with my limited human mind; however, I know that on the cosmic level, I must be in the right place, at the right time, doing the right thing. Positive thoughts are what I choose to think. This present experience is a stepping-stone to a new awareness and greater glory.

# I give thanks
# each and
# every day

I am grateful for all of the wonderful things in my world—the beautiful daffodils, the delicious food, the computers and other technological wonders that make my life easier, my good friends, my lovely home, my sleek car, my loving pets, my intelligent mind, my healthy body—everything! I express gratitude to the Universe often, knowing that my thoughts are heard and appreciated. I have a perpetual attitude of gratitude.

# I forgive everyone, including myself

When I hold on to the past with bitterness and anger and don't allow myself to experience the present moment, I am wasting today. If I hold on to bitterness and grudges for a long time, it has to do with forgiving myself, not the other person. If I hold on to old hurts, I punish myself in the here and now. I no longer want to sit in a prison of self-righteous resentment. I decide that I'd rather be happy than always right. I forgive myself and stop punishing myself.

# I rejoice
## in my
## employment

My job is to express Life. I rejoice in this employment. I give thanks for every opportunity to demonstrate the power of Divine Intelligence to work through me. Any time I am presented with a challenge, I know it is an opportunity from Life, my employer, and I quiet my intellect, turn within, and wait for words of treatment to fill my mind. I accept these blessed revelations with joy and know that I am worthy of my just rewards for a job well done. In exchange for this exhilarating job, I am abundantly compensated. My fellow employees—all of humankind—are supportive, loving, cheerful, enthusiastic, and powerful workers in the field of spiritual unfoldment, and we bless each other with love.

# I get rid of the "shoulds" in my life

I remove the word *should* from my vocabulary forever. *Should* is a word that makes a prisoner of me. Every time I say *should*, I am making myself wrong, or I am making someone else wrong. I am, in effect, saying, *I am not good enough.* From hereon in, I replace the word *should* with the word *could*. *Could* lets me know that I have choice, and choice is freedom. I need to be aware that everything I do in life is done by choice. There is really nothing that I *have* to do. I always have choice.

# I sleep peacefully

Sleep is a time to restore myself and wrap up the day. My body repairs itself and becomes renewed and refreshed. My mind moves into the dream state where the problems of the day are sorted out. I prepare myself for the new day ahead. As I enter the sleep state, I take positive thoughts with me—thoughts that create a wonderful new day and a wonderful new future. So if there is any anger or blame in me, I let it go. If there is any resentment or fear, I let it go. If there is any jealousy or rage, I let it go. If there is any guilt or need for punishment lingering in the corners of my mind, I let it go. I feel only peace in my mind and body as I drift off to sleep.

I am
healthy
and
filled with
energy

I know and affirm that my body is a friendly place to live. I have respect for my body, and I treat it well. I nourish it with good foods and healthy exercise. I affirm positive things about my body and tell it I love it often. I connect with the energy of the Universe, and I allow it to flow through me. I have wonderful energy. I am radiant, vital, and alive!

# There is a solution to every problem

For every problem I create, there is a solution. I am not limited by my human-mind thinking, for I am connected with the entire Universal Wisdom and Knowledge. I come from the loving space of the heart and know that love opens all doors. There is an ever-ready Power that helps me meet and overcome every challenge and crisis in my life. I know that every problem has been healed somewhere in the world. Therefore, I know that this can happen for me. I wrap myself in a cocoon of love, and know that all is well in my world.

# Infinite spirit
# is eternal

I know that the sun is always shining. Even though clouds may come along and obscure the sun for a while, the sun is always shining. The sun never stops shining. And even though the earth turns and the sun appears to go down, it never really stops shining. The same is true of Infinite Power and Infinite Spirit. It is eternal. It is always here, always giving light to me. I may obscure its presence by the clouds of negative thinking, but that Spirit, that Power, that healing energy, is always with me.

I am
on an endless
journey
through
eternity

In the infinity of life, all is perfect, whole, and complete. The cycle of life is also perfect, whole, and complete. There is a time of beginning, a time of growth, a time of being, a time of withering or wearing out, and a time of leaving. This is all part of the perfection of life. I sense it as normal and natural, and though saddened at times, I accept the cycle and its rhythms. Sometimes there is an abrupt ending in mid-cycle. I am jarred and feel threatened. Someone dies too soon, or something was smashed and broken. However, I know that life is ever-changing. There is no beginning and no end, only a constant cycling and recycling of substance and experience. Life is never stuck or static or stale, for each moment is ever-new and fresh. Every ending is a new point of beginning.

# I dwell on positive thoughts

Thoughts are like drops of water. When I think the same thoughts over and over again, I am creating this incredible body of water. First, I have a little puddle, then I may get a pond, and as I continue to think the same thoughts over and over and over again, I have a lake, and finally an ocean. If my thoughts are negative, I can drown in a sea of my own negativity. If my thoughts are positive, I can float on the ocean of life.

# I am here at the right time

I am on an endless journey through eternity, and the time I spend on this plane of reality is but a brief instant. I choose to come to this planet to learn lessons, to work on my spiritual growth, and to expand my capacity to love. There is no right time and no wrong time to come and go. I always come in during the middle of the movie, and I leave during the middle of the movie. I leave when my particular task is finished. I come to learn to love myself more and to share that love with all those around me. I come to open my heart on a much deeper level. My capacity to love is the only thing I take with me when I leave.

I love all
that I have created
for myself

I love and accept myself exactly as I am. I support myself and trust myself wherever I am. I place my hand over my heart and feel the love that is in there. I know that there is plenty of room for me to accept myself right here and now. I accept my body, my weight, my height, my appearance, my sexuality, and my experiences. I accept all that I have created for myself—my past and present. I am willing to allow my future to happen. I am a Divine, magnificent expression of life, and I deserve the very best. I accept this for myself now. I accept miracles. I accept healing. I accept wholeness. And most of all, I accept myself. I am precious, and I cherish who I am.

# I love and accept myself right now

I love myself in this very moment—I don't wait until I lose the weight, get a new job, find a lover, or whatever. This moment is my reality, and I know that the only time I can begin to love who I am is right here and right now. Unconditional love is love with no expectations or conditions. It is the way I choose to love myself. It is accepting what is.

# I am one with everyone on the planet

I do not believe in two powers of good and evil. I think that there is One Infinite Spirit, and there are human beings who have the opportunity to use the intelligence and wisdom and tools they have been given in every way. When I say *they,* I am really talking about *me,* because I am the people, I am the government, I am the churches, and I am the planet. The place to begin making changes is right where I am. I think it is all too easy to say, *It's the devil. It's them.* It is really always *me!*

I perceive
my true
being

I see myself having a consciousness of oneness with the presence and power of God. My wisdom and understanding of Spirit increases, and I express the inner beauty and strength of my true being. Divine order is ever-present in my experience, and there is plenty of time for all that I choose to do. I express wisdom, understanding, and love in all of my dealings with others, and my words are Divinely guided. I see myself expressing the creative energy of Spirit in my work, my writing, and my speech. Fun, uplifting ideas flow through my consciousness, and I follow through on the ideas received, bringing them into full manifestation.

# I am my own unique self

I am not my father. I am not my mother. I am not any of my relatives. I am not my teachers at school, nor am I the limitations of my early religious training. I am myself. I am special and unique, with my own set of talents and abilities. No one can do things exactly the way I can do them. There is no competition and no comparison. I am worthy of my own love and my own self-acceptance. I am a magnificent being. I am free. I acknowledge this as the new truth for myself.

# I am a natural winner

As I learn to love myself, I become powerful. My love for myself moves me from being a victim to being a winner. My love for myself attracts wonderful experiences. People who feel good about themselves are naturally attractive because they have an aura about them that is just wonderful. They are always winning at life. I am willing to learn to love myself now. I am a winner, too.

I freely
express
who I am

I am indeed blessed. There are wonderful opportunities to be myself, to express who I really am. I am the beauty and joy of the Universe, expressing and receiving. I surround myself with Divine honesty and justice. I know that Divine right action is taking place, and whatever the outcome is, it is perfect for me and everyone concerned. I am one with the very power that created me. I am wonderful. I rejoice in the truth of my being. I accept it as so and let it be. I say, *So be it,* and I know that all is well in my wonderful world right here and right now.

# I trust the Intelligence within me

There is One Intelligence. It is everywhere, omnipresent. This Intelligence is within me and is in everything that I am looking for. When I get lost or lose something, I don't start saying, *I am in the wrong place, I won't find my way.* I know that nothing is ever lost in the Divine Mind. I completely trust the Intelligence within me to guide me to the right path.

# I am part of the harmonious whole

I am a Divine idea expressing through the One Mind in harmonious ways. Everything I do is based on the one truth—the truth of my being and the truth of life. Divine right action is guiding me every moment of the day. I say the right word at the right time and follow the right course of action at all times. I am part of the harmonious whole, as we all are. There is a Divine blending of energies as people work joyfully together, supporting and encouraging each other in ways that are fulfilling and productive. I am healthy, happy, loving, joyful, respectful, supportive, productive, and at peace with myself and with others.

Not everyone has the special family that I have, nor do they have the extra opportunities to open their hearts in the way my family does. I am not limited by what the neighbors think or by society's prejudices. I am far more than that. I have a family that comes from love, and I accept with pride every unique member. I am special, and I am worthy of love. I love and accept each member of my wonderful family, and they, in turn, love and adore me. I am safe. All is well in my world.

I am
willing to
change and
grow

I am willing to learn new things because I know that I do not know it all. I am willing to drop old concepts when they no longer work for me. I am willing to see situations about myself and say: *I don't want to do that anymore.* I know I can become more of who I am—not a better person, because that implies that I am not good enough, but I can become *more* of who I am. Growing and changing is exciting, even if I have to look at some painful things inside myself in order to do it.

# I follow my inner wisdom

My inner wisdom knows all of the answers. Sometimes it is scary to know that, because the answer I get inside may be quite different from what my friends or family want me to do. Yet I know inwardly what is right for me, and if I follow this inner wisdom, I am at peace with my own being. I support myself in making the right choices for me. When I am in doubt, I ask myself: *Am I coming from the loving space of the heart? Is this a decision that is loving for me? Is this right for me now?* The decision I make at some later point—a day, a week, or a month later— may no longer be the right choice, and then I can change it. I ask in every moment: *Is this right for me?* And I reply: *I love myself, and I am making the right choices.*

# This world is my heaven on earth

In this new millennium, I see a community of spiritually minded souls who come together to share, grow, and radiate their energies into the world—each one free to pursue his or her individual purpose. I help create a world where the nurturing of soul growth is the most important activity, and where this is the work of the individual. There is ample time and opportunity for creative expression in whatever area I choose. There will be no undue concern with respect to earning money. All that I need I will be able to express through the powers within. Education will be a process of remembering that which I already know and bring to conscious awareness. There is no dis-ease, no poverty, no crime, and no deceit. The world of the future begins now, right here, with all of us. And so it is.

# By Louise L. Hay

Self Healing
Songs of Affirmation
    (with Joshua Leeds)
Tools for Success
What I Believe/Deep
    Relaxation
You Can Heal Your Life
    (audio book)
You Can Heal Your Life
    Study Course

**Conversations on Living
Lecture Series**
Change and Transition
Dissolving Barriers
The Forgotten Child Within
How to Love Yourself
The Power of Your
    Spoken Word
Receiving Prosperity
Totality of Possibilities
Your Thoughts Create
    Your Life

**Personal Power Through
Imagery Series**
Anger Releasing
Forgiveness/Loving the
    Inner Child

**Subliminal Mastery
Series**
Feeling Fine Affirmations
Love Your Body
    Affirmations
Safe Driving Affirmations
Self-Esteem Affirmations
Self-Healing Affirmations
Stress-Free Affirmations

**CDs**
Self-Healing
Forgiveness/Loving the
    Inner Child & Anger
    Releasing
Meditations for Personal
Healing/Overcoming Fears
Self-Esteem Affirmations

**VIDEOCASSETTES**
Dissolving Barriers
Doors Opening: A Positive
    Approach to Aids
Receiving Prosperity
You Can Heal Your Life
    Study Course
Your Thoughts Create
    Your Life

**ALSO AVAILABLE**
Power Thought Cards
Wisdom Cards

*All of the above can be
ordered through your local
bookstore, or call or fax:*
**(800) 654-5126**
**(800) 650-5115 (fax)**

Please visit the Hay House
Website at: **hayhouse.com**

# About the Author

**Louise L. Hay** is a metaphysical lecturer and teacher and the bestselling author of 24 books, including *You Can Heal Your Life* and *Empowering Women.* Her works have been translated into 25 different languages in 33 countries throughout the world. Since beginning her career as a Science of Mind minister in 1981, Louise has assisted thousands of people in discovering and using the full potential of their own creative powers for personal growth and self-healing. Louise is the owner and founder of Hay House, Inc., a self-help publishing company that disseminates books, audios, and videos that contribute to the healing of the planet.

# HAY HOUSE
# Lifestyles Titles

## Flip Books

*101 Ways to Happiness*, by Louise L. Hay
*101 Ways to Health and Healing*,
    by Louise L. Hay
*101 Ways to Romance*,
    by Barbara De Angelis, Ph.D.
*101 Ways to Transform My Life*,
    by Dr. Wayne W. Dyer

## Books

*A Garden of Thoughts*, by Louise L. Hay
*Aromatherapy A–Z*, by Connie Higley,
    Alan Higley, and Pat Leatham
*Aromatherapy 101*, by Karen Downes
*Colors & Numbers*, by Louise L. Hay
*Constant Craving A–Z*, by Doreen Virtue, Ph.D.
*Dream Journal*, by Leon Nacson
*Healing with Herbs and Home Remedies A–Z*,
    by Hanna Kroeger
*Healing with the Angels Oracle Cards* (booklet
    and card pack), by Doreen Virtue, Ph.D.
*Heal Your Body A–Z*, by Louise L. Hay
*Home Design with Feng Shui A–Z*,
    by Terah Kathryn Collins

*Homeopathy A–Z*, by Dana Ullman, M.P.H.
*Inner Wisdom,* by Louise L. Hay
*Interpreting Dreams A–Z*, by Leon Nacson
*Meditations,* by Sylvia Browne
*Natural Gardening A–Z*, by Donald W. Trotter
*Natural Healing for Dogs and Cats A–Z,*
    by *Cheryl Schwartz*, D.V.M.
*Natural Pregnancy A–Z,*
    by Carolle Jean-Murat, M.D.
*Pleasant Dreams*, by Amy E. Dean
*Weddings A–Z*, by Deborah McCoy
*What Color Is Your Personality?*
    by Carol Ritberger, Ph.D.
*What Is Spirit?,* by Lexie Brockway Potamkin
*You Can Heal Your Life*, by Louise L. Hay

and

*Power Thought Cards,*
    by Louise L. Hay (affirmation cards)

All of the above titles may be ordered by calling
Hay House at the numbers on the last page.

We hope you enjoyed
this Hay House Lifestyles book.
If you would like to receive a free catalog
featuring additional Hay House books and
products, or if you would like information
about the Hay Foundation, please contact:

Hay House, Inc.
P.O. Box 5100
Carlsbad, CA 92018-5100

**(760) 431-7695** or **(800) 654-5126**
**(760) 431-6948 (fax)** or **(800) 650-5115 (fax)**

Please visit the Hay House Website at:
**hayhouse.com**